THE GAME

THE GAME

A ROOKIE FIREFIGHTER'S
MANUAL FOR SUCCESS

RENICK SAMPSON

Printed in the United States of America

First Printing, 2017

WANT TO KNOW WHAT IT'S REALLY LIKE TO BE A ROOKIE FIREFIGHTER?

With over twenty years of experience, Renick Sampson will prepare you for the many roles and expectations of a rookie firefighter, and will explain the different points that are critical to your success during probation. After reading *The Game*, you'll be ready to start your career with the knowledge of an experienced firefighter in your back pocket.

FROM THE AUTHOR:

"I saw a hole in the way future firefighters here in the United States prepare for their careers. All of the focus is on developing skills and tactics. And even though those tools allow a firefighter to be successful at the scene of an emergency, very few rookies understand what is expected of them when they show up to the station for their first shift. There is little to no rookie expectation training and many probationary firefighters are not able to learn their role in the firehouse fast enough. This leads to added stress, issues during probation, and possibly even termination for those who can't keep up."

Don't enter your hard-earned career blind! Read *The Game*—be prepared!

PREFACE

It's early morning as I pull into the parking lot behind the station for the first time. I open the door of my beat-up Ford Bronco and step outside, pulling my heavy gear bag out of the back seat. It's cold out, and as I walk toward the rear bay doors, I notice the morning dew still on the ground. My stomach is full of nerves. As I approach the station, the alarm sounds. My heart races as I scramble to get ready. The engine starts to pull out of the station as I jump on board. I introduce myself to the crew—and my long-anticipated fire career begins.

That was the scenario I played over and over again in my head. It most likely came from a movie, but that made no difference to me. All I wanted to do was fight fire.

TABLE OF CONTENTS

INTRODUCTION

"Challenge accepted"

B ESIDES the adrenaline, there are two reasons why most of us want to be involved in the fire service. First, there is something inside that draws us to the service of others. Helping people when they are at their lowest is probably the number-one reason people pursue this career. Second is the idea of being part of the "fire family"; feeling like no matter what happens, you have a group of people that you trust with your life. It's the feeling you get hanging out at the kitchen table in the morning, talking with the crew over a cup of coffee after running calls all night, or getting to know each other's families during holiday parties and weekend get-togethers. The fact that you are living with your crew turns coworkers into family.

Wanting to help people is the easy part. While everyone in the fire service has this common characteristic, the hard part is actually *making it happen*. Attaining your goal of becoming a firefighter means working tirelessly until you are given the opportunity to prove yourself.

EARNING YOUR JOB

THE fire service is a highly sought-after profession. It takes a great deal of family support, financial investment, and time to prepare for a fire career, which makes it clear why firefighting breeds such a highly competitive and emotional job market. It is common for a hiring fire department to receive thousands of applications. It's your responsibility to make yourself more marketable than your competition. Here is a very simple equation you need to know in order to stand apart from the crowd and get yourself a job offer:

Outstanding resume + testing skills + physical fitness + great interview skills =
Job offer

If getting hired has been a struggle for you, it may be because you're lacking part of this equation. You need to do a self-assessment and do everything in your power to improve in any troubled areas. No one is going to do this for you!

Some examples may include:

- Have a professional review your resume.

- Take a remedial math or reading-comprehension class.

- Start working with a physical trainer and improve your diet.

- Video yourself answering interview questions and work on your body language.

- Do mock oral interviews with anyone who will sit down with you.

There are other parts of the hiring process as well, such as the psychological exam, the polygraph, and the background investigation. These tests are just as important to you getting hired as the equation mentioned earlier, but they aren't things you can actively prepare for, or change your ability to succeed in over a short period of time.

It can take years of practice in each testable area to rise to the level of being a hirable candidate and ultimately getting that job offer. But when it happens, it's a very exciting time and something you will never forget!

SO, YOU GOT A JOB OFFER...

Congratulations on getting hired! Sort of.

Here's the thing most people don't realize. While getting a job offer is a huge step in the right direction, it's still just a step in the process. *Everything you do from the time you submit your application until the time your probationary period ends is all part of the hiring process.* Most fire departments have a twelve-month probationary period, though some may be up to eighteen months. This means in order to successfully complete your probation and become a career firefighter, you first need to be an effective rookie every shift for up to a year and a half. To accomplish that, you must learn your job and your role in the fire service. To be a successful rookie, you need to know how to play **the game**.

A game is defined by Merriam-Webster's dictionary as an "activity engaged in for diversion or amusement." But in the fire service, "the game" is not a form of diversion or amusement at all. In fact, it is a way of life.

For a rookie firefighter, the game should be defined as, "meeting the expectations of the members of your department by having a respectful, hard working, can-do attitude."

Most firefighters in the United States begin their journey at a fire academy. This is where you learn the basics of the game. In the academy you will address everyone as "Sir" or "Ma'am," do the housework, and learn how to follow orders. But the fire academy's main objective is to embed in you the skills needed to do the physical aspects of the job. Your instructors will teach you how to pull hose, throw ladders, and ventilate a building, along with many other necessary skills that allow you to do your job in a safe and efficient manner, achieve tactical goals, and ultimately go home to your loved ones at the end of every shift.

Academy life is very rigid. The rules and objectives are clear, and there is little left for interpretation. Station life is different. Station life is where the game gets complicated.

How you decide to play the game during your probation will define how the department views you for the rest of your career. If you play properly, you will grow into a well-rounded, respected, hard-working, useful rookie. Your crew will be willing to help mold you. They will take a prideful ownership in how well you are progressing, wanting to teach you what they know. On the flip side, if you do not play well, your life can become very difficult. The dream of going to work as a rookie firefighter can quickly become nothing more than stress and misery.

WHO AM I?

BY now, you might be wondering who I am and how I'm qualified to help you.

I have spent years helping countless firefighters make the transition from academy life to volunteer firefighter, and then on to full-time firefighter. I have been involved with the game in one way or another for the past two decades. I currently hold the position of engineer with a municipal fire department in Southern California. I also coordinate my department's Auxiliary Reserve program, where it is my responsibility to take academy graduates and prepare them for the life of a rookie firefighter.

I decided to write this book because I saw a hole in the way future firefighters here in the United States prepare for their careers. All of the focus is on developing skills and tactics. And even though those tools allow us to be successful at the scene of an emergency, very few rookie firefighters understand what is expected of them when they show up to the station for their first shift. There is little to no rookie expectation training and many probationary firefighters are not able to learn their role in the firehouse fast enough. This leads to added stress, issues during probation, and possibly even termination for those who can't keep up.

This book will bridge the gap between academy life and station life by giving you insight into what is expected of a rookie firefighter. I truly hope that everyone—from the person just starting to explore a career in firefighting, to the experienced firefighter who may just need a little extra advice—will be able to pull something useful from my experiences.

THE FIVE POINTS

OVER the years, I have learned that there are five key components, or points, to a rookie's job. They are: character, station duties, testing, chow, and emergency response. Learning how to navigate each point is critical to your success as a rookie firefighter. I will also tell you from experience that this task is never easy.

CHARACTER

"Career mode"

THE three words that should define a rookie are **attitude, effort, and teamwork**. These are the personal characteristics that a fire department will look for in a recruit, for the simple fact that these are unteachable traits. These three character traits are instilled very early in life and are reinforced through years of personal experiences. Your character will prove to be important when you start interacting with the other firefighters in your department—the other players in the game. Even though the fire service is a highly diverse group, we typically have a common core set of values. When you have these three characteristics in common with the other players, it will make your interactions with them all the more successful.

THE PLAYERS

JUST as in any game, the players are split into different teams. The fire service is no different. The two teams in this game are: The Experienced (home team) versus the Newcomers (visitors).

THE HOME TEAM

HISTORICALLY, firefighting jobs have been given to people who have had experience working with their hands for a living. They may have backgrounds in construction, the military, or other fields that require physical labor. They are able to pull from their life experiences in order to know what will work on an emergency scene and what will not. Most became firefighters because they enjoy hard work, figuring out problems, and being a benefit to society. Some of them still run successful businesses on their days off. Most of these individuals were hired with little to no college experience. They were not paramedics when they were hired, just hard workers. Many went back to school on their own and successfully graduated from college later in their careers.

BONUS TIP

Remember that the people who used to mop the floors of your station are now in charge of your training and development. To succeed, you need to realize that they have already been in your position and that they understand what it takes to be a good rookie.

THE VISITORS

FOR the new generation of firefighters, the reason for wanting to be involved with the fire service is usually the same as it was for the older generations, but society's expectations regarding college and our own hiring processes have changed the fire service. Most new hires have a different background from the older generations of firefighters. They may have worked on ambulances and/or have gone directly to college after high school, where they probably received a four-year degree in a field of study that has very little to do with firefighting.

As a rookie firefighter, until you can prove everyone wrong, it is assumed that what you know about physical labor and working as a member of a team has come straight out of a book. This is a problem because firefighting is an extremely physical job that requires one hundred percent team participation for us to be successful.

This next section may not apply to you personally, but you need to understand that some rookies have entitlement issues. They feel like they deserve more than they have earned. It is important to be aware that you are not doing us any favors by merely showing up. We don't give out participation trophies, and we don't owe you anything. Lives are on the line and we take that seriously. Your position as a firefighter needs to be earned through hard work and discipline.

SURVIVAL

Now that you have been introduced to the players in the game and understand what you are up against, let's take a look at how you can enter this challenge and make it out the other side with your job still in hand.

The first thing you need in order to survive the game is the right **mentality**. As a rookie, your approach should be, "Until I am off probation and accepted by the crew:

- I am a guest in their house.

- I will respect the rules and traditions of their house and do everything in my power to make life easier for my hosts.

- I will not be a noisy guest.

- I will stay humble and appreciative.

- I will keep my appearance clean and respectful.

- I will do what I can to lighten the workload for everyone.

- I will keep my hands out of my pockets.

- I will keep my opinion to myself.

- I will keep my head down.

- I will keep my eyes and ears open so I can learn from the experience around me.

- I will absolutely try my hardest, always."

This strategy will keep you working hard and out of trouble with your crew, but that's only a small part of surviving the game. Your main goal is to get your crew to feel invested in you and your work. You want the crew to be in your corner and interested in your progression along the way.

So, here's a good question: How do you begin a new career with a group of people who are like family to each other and convince them to take you in and treat you like one of their own? How do you get them to teach you the ways of the fire service and pass on years and years of experience and tradition to you?

GET EXCITED!

You need to act interested in your new position and get excited. And in order to achieve that, there are a few simple things you need to do:

- Carry a positive mental attitude about everything.
- Ask lots and lots of questions.
- Listen and *follow through* with what people recommend—don't just let their words go in one ear and out the other.
- Don't correct people unless it's a safety issue. You don't want to be the rookie who is telling the twenty-year veteran how to "do it the right way."
- Gratefully accept criticism of any type and turn it into constructive criticism.
- Show up every day with a smile on your face.
- If they feed you a shit sandwich, eat every bite, smile, and ask for another.

People will line up to help someone who wants to learn. People get invested in someone they have taught. They want you to do a good job because that means they did a good job in leading you. That's how you win over a crew and gain a good reputation. That's the secret to becoming a part of the firehouse family.

ROOKIE DO'S AND DON'TS

As a rookie, your reputation will spread like wildfire. This starts with your first impression, which can have either a positive or negative impact on your probation. And since we are trying to minimize the negative, be aware that nothing bothers people in the fire service more than a new rookie who acts too comfortable.

So, in order to start out with the right foot forward, here is a list of do's and don'ts you should read before your first day:

- **Do** introduce yourself to everyone. Be sure to speak up and make eye contact when you do.

- **Do** perfect the solid handshake. Not too aggressive, but no dead fish.

- **Do** keep yourself looking sharp. Attention to detail and your image go a long way in the fire service.

- **Do** ask whether a seat at the dining table is available before sitting for your first few meals with a new crew. You're a guest and you don't want to take someone's favorite seat.

- **Do** be the last to sit for a meal and the first up to clean.

- **Do** learn how to make a pot of coffee.

- **Don't** drink coffee at the station in the morning. Drinking coffee in the morning implies that you have nothing better to do, and as a rookie you should always have something to do. If you need a cup of morning coffee, then drink it on your way to work and save yourself some grief.

- **Don't** lean against the counters. "If there's time to lean, there's time to clean!"

- **Don't** watch TV or sit around reading the paper. As with drinking coffee, you should have more important things to do.

- **Don't** use profanity, even though it seems like everyone else is. You don't know your audience yet and you need to keep up your professional image, especially in public.

- **Don't** sit in the La-Z-Boy chairs.

- **Don't** eat dessert unless invited for a special occasion.

- **Don't** put your hands in your pockets.

- **Don't** chew on toothpicks, wear sunglasses, or eat sunflower seeds.

CELL PHONES

OBVIOUSLY, cell phone use is not on the decline. As a rookie, you need to be aware of cell phone etiquette and of how using your device will be viewed by others. Cell phone usage by a rookie is a tricky thing. It falls into the same time-wasting category as drinking coffee, reading the newspaper, and watching television.

With that being said, a phone can also be a valuable tool when it is used for studying fire-related materials, taking pictures of equipment to study at home, looking up pertinent information while on an emergency, or even helping the engineer locate a hard to find address.

There is no doubt that a phone can be both a benefit and a suck on your productivity. The issue is how others perceive you while you are using it. If you use it appropriately and sparingly it will not be an issue. But if you use it constantly for the wrong reasons, then it *will* be a problem. Use common sense!

There are a few areas where cell phone usage draws more negative attention than others. You should play the game and avoid the following situations:

- Never pull out a cell phone during a class. Period.

- Riding in the back of the engine after a call is no time to text your BFF. That's the time to think about the call you're returning from and ask questions like, "What could I have done differently?" and, "Why was that call ALS criteria and the other hypertension call wasn't?" It's the time to think about that apartment building you're passing by and wonder, "What is the distance to the back of that deep lot? How much hose would be needed if that building were to catch fire? Where is the nearest hydrant? Does that old furniture store have a sprinkler system? Is there a standpipe in that nursing home?"

- Stay away from social media while on duty. Not only are you telling everyone that you are on your phone doing nondepartmental business while on the clock, but doing so may also be against department policy and could get you into trouble.

Finally, there is the simple fact that your expensive phone could get crushed on a response or destroyed by a well-placed water drop. So make it easy on yourself and leave your cell phone in your locker or in the apparatus you are riding on for that day.

THE PRIVILEGE OF SERVICE

FIREFIGHTING in the United States has a deep history of tradition and public respect. This foundation of pride and trust in the fire service was earned through the blood, sweat, and tears of everyone who has worn the badge before you. It's now your turn to uphold the same ideology that got us to where we are today.

Whether you are already a probationary firefighter or are still looking forward to it, I can assure you that probation will be one of the most difficult and rewarding experiences of your life. And no matter how tough your probation is, you need to realize how lucky you are to have this opportunity. There are thousands of people out there who would love to take your position. Stay focused on your goal of becoming a career firefighter and the accomplishments and lifestyle you are working so hard for will soon be yours, if you are able to successfully play the game.

STATION DUTIES

"Big points"

THERE is a saying in the firehouse: "Your mom doesn't work here." I'm sorry to break it to you, but for *your* first couple of years, *our* mom does work here—and it's you.

Let me explain. First of all, I don't believe a mother's role is to pick up after her kids. I believe it is to raise children into adults who are able to take care of themselves. I also don't believe that the purpose of a rookie is to pick up after his or her crew. We are all adults and should be expected to do this for ourselves (if our moms taught us right).

However, station duties are a major component of playing the game and one of the best ways to showcase your work ethic. Station duties can be described as "work that is done on a daily basis to keep the firehouse and equipment functioning." This includes equipment checks, station and vehicle maintenance, meals, and any other vital tasks that are completed daily.

I have witnessed many situations where station duties were the first problem during someone's probation. If you are not doing your duties to the expectations of the crew, you will quickly be labeled as an unmotivated slow mover, also known as a "slug." Once this happens, you can be sure your crew will be looking for any reason to come down on you.

Let's take a look at how the station duties fall into the daily routine of a rookie firefighter.

THE ROOKIE'S DAILY ROUTINE

EACH fire department will have its own daily routine, but the schedule below will give you the general idea. This schedule is for a twenty-four- or forty-eight-hour shift with a 0630 shift change.

0545

- Arrive at station
- Change into uniform or PT gear
- Secure all personal protective equipment and place it on your apparatus for the day

Arriving at least forty-five minutes prior to shift change allows you enough time to prepare for your shift. It is a courtesy to the person you will be relieving from duty. If an emergency call comes in during that time, you will be able to respond in their place, allowing them to leave on time.

0600

- Start coffee

Always make sure there is a fresh pot of coffee brewing before people start to wake up. If you don't, you will probably hear the coffee pot come crashing down the hall-way. We call that "bowling for rookies."

0615

- Walk station grounds for trash
- Open blinds and gates
- Bring in newspaper and lay it out nicely

You will want to get all the quiet tasks done during this time. Always open and shut doors quietly out of respect for those still sleeping.

0630

- Shift change
- Coffee check

This is the time to exchange information with the previous shift on anything pertinent to your upcoming shift.

0700

- Empty dishwasher
- Coffee check

For some reason, dishes make an unnatural amount of noise. Be very careful about putting dishes away when people may be sleeping.

0710

Apparatus equipment check:
- Radio batteries
- Breathers
- Medical gloves
- EMS forms
- Hand tools
- EMS equipment
- Rig inventory
- Start all power tools

It's your responsibility to do a good inventory check on your apparatus and start any power tools assigned to that rig. If any equipment is needed later that day and is found missing or non-operational, the fallout will land on you. For the first few weeks, you should probably do this under the supervision of the engineer or senior firefighter on your shift until they are comfortable with you doing it by yourself.

0730

- Coffee check
- Continue apparatus checks

Check coffee every 30 minutes in the morning.

0800

- Morning meeting
- Coffee Check

Each morning, you may have a shift meeting. You should always stand during the meetings until asked to sit. Have a notepad ready to write down anything that needs to be done that day. This is the point where you should bring up any rookie sign-offs, company schools, or tests you have for that day. This enables the Station Captain to schedule your needs into the day. This is also a good time to volunteer to handle the chow plans.

0830

- Fitness

The hour of power! Use common sense here. If you have a gym at your station and it's crowded, then do something else like squats or pull-ups outside, go for a run around the block (with a radio and your Captain's approval), or jump rope. You don't want to crowd out the older guys in the gym. Also, make sure you use good gym etiquette. Don't go around dropping weights and don't leave your machines all sweaty! That's nasty.

0930

- Dressed for the day

Station maintenance:
- Clean the bathrooms, including mirrors, toilets, sinks, floors, and counters
- Take out all of the garbage
- Vacuum the entire station
- Give the kitchen a quick clean

As the rookie, you should be the first one showered up and in uniform. It's also a good idea to keep a power bar or some type of quick breakfast in your locker.

There isn't much time here for station maintenance, so you should do this as quickly as you can while still doing a good job. Make sure you complete these tasks every day, even if you have to come back later in the day and finish. This is one area where your work ethic will be on display.

For more on this, see Sampson's Housework Tips, page 24.

Weekly duty (example):

- Monday—Clean showers
- Tuesday—Wash all support vehicles
- Wednesday—Decon and clean gym
- Thursday—Detail the kitchen
- Friday—Clean offices and dorms
- Saturday—Yard work

Some firehouses also have a weekly duty. Mine did. We would detail out one portion of the station every day.

There is no time slot here because different duties may be done at different times.

For example, we always detailed out the kitchen after dinner so it was nice and clean for the oncoming shift.

1030

- Shop for lunch or
- morning training session

Some days, training in the morning will keep you from being able to shop for lunch, so you may have to eat out.

1100

- Prepare lunch

Try your hardest to have lunch ready on time so everyone can maximize their break.

1200

- Lunch

Remember, you should be the last to sit...

1230

- Lunch clean up

...and the first up to start cleaning.

1245

Quiet time:
- Collect the mail from the front door
- Prepare for a company school or test
- **Quietly** go over some equipment that you are not familiar with

After lunch, most firefighters take advantage of a small window of time to take a break. You may see people reading, catching up on emails, or taking a quick "safety" nap. This time is sacred to firefighters and should not be interrupted unless there is an emergency.

1325

- Coffee

This might be a good time to make a pot.

1330

Flexible time:
- Station projects
- Fire prevention inspections
- Target hazard walkthroughs
- Rookie drills

If nothing has been planned for the afternoon, you should find yourself a project to complete. For ideas, see the list of Time Killers on page 24.

1600

- Shop for dinner

Unless you were able to do it during your lunch shopping trip.

1630

- Close blinds and gates
- Turn on the exterior lights

After your department's business day has come to a close, you need to prepare for the night.

1700

- Prepare dinner

This is a time where most people congregate in the kitchen and help with the cooking.

1800

- Dinner

Everyone's favorite part of the day.

1830

- Clean up

Not everyone's favorite part of the day. That's why you should be the first one up to start cleaning.

1900

- Tally the chow bill
- Coffee

For details on this, see the Chow chapter, page 37.

1930

- Make your "fart sack" for the night
- Wipe down your rig, with permission from your engineer

A fart sack is what my department calls your bedding. Don't forget yours or I can guarantee a miserable night. Trust me on this. I've done it.

2000

- Personal study time
- Extra work out

This time frame should be used for more studying, going over equipment, or getting an extra workout in.

When it comes to the extra workout, you need to be certain all other tasks for the day have been completed. Even then, you need to confirm that it is acceptable with your senior firefighter or supervisor before working out. You don't want to do anything considered personal before all of your work has been done.

2200

- Close down the station
- Close out the chow box
- Walk the station for used cups and misplaced items
- Do a quick tidy of the kitchen
- Prepare the coffee for the morning
- Start the dishwasher
- Secure all the station doors and vehicles

You want the station to be prepared for the morning. It will save you time and is considered a point of pride to have the station in good condition when the next shift comes on duty.

The station security also falls on your shoulders, so make sure to lock it up.

2300–0000

- Shower up
- Bedtime

Using a personal alarm is a tricky thing in the fire service. If you have a shared dorm room, you can feel pretty confident that if your alarm wakes up the entire crew at 0530, they will not be happy about it. So here's what I recommend. Take that cell phone out of your locker. Make sure it is on vibrate only. Slide it into your pillowcase and all the way to the far side, away from the opening. This way, you won't disturb anyone when your alarm goes off and you won't lose it in the middle of the night and oversleep. Also, make sure you turn off that annoying hourly beep on your watch!

DAY 2

0545

- Wake up
- Start coffee
- Give turnover report to oncoming firefighter
- Go home

If your department works twenty-four-hour shifts, then you can leave after you give your turnover report to your relief. If you work forty-eight-hour shifts, you get to stay and do the entire routine over again.

SAMPSON'S HOUSEWORK TIPS

As I mentioned earlier, housework is a major component of the game. Here are some subtle tips that will make your work noticeable:

- Leave the blue water in the toilets after they have been scrubbed down. That removes all doubt about whether they have been cleaned or not.

- I have seen others fold the toilet paper into a little triangle at the end to show they have been there. I wish I had thought of that!

- Don't be afraid to vacuum areas where people are working. Just be sure to ask if the noise will bother them before you start.

- Keep an eye out for loose change behind doors and under recliners. Some people use coins as indicators to see whether the vacuuming has been done. I would always count and leave the change stacked neatly on the kitchen counter. Count it just in case someone asks how much change you found that day.

TIME KILLERS

EVERYONE imagines that a day as a firefighter is full of excitement and danger. The truth is, sometimes it is and sometimes it isn't. As a rookie on those not-so-exciting days, you still need to be productive. Here are some time-killing projects for those long afternoons that most rookies overlook. Remember, "If there's time to lean, there's time to clean!"

- Refill empty oxygen and SCBA bottles. This task has priority over the others on the list and shouldn't be considered just a time killer if your supply is getting low.

- Spend a few hours cleaning air conditioner vents or light fixtures.

- Walk the station grounds again and look for trash. Clean the trash out of the gutters across the street too. Nobody likes looking at trash.

- Take care of graffiti on your station, or if your city has a graffiti removal hotline, you can call them. You can also call it for your neighbors.

- Wipe down vehicles, but never dry rub a vehicle! If the vehicle is very dirty or you are unsure, ask your engineer first.

- Wash, dry, and fold the station towels used for drying the rigs.

- Wash windows. You can *always* wash windows.

- Pull weeds out of the cracks in the concrete.

- Sweep anything that needs to be swept.

- Scrape gum off the apparatus floor.

- Repaint hand tools, organize the shop toolbox, or sharpen axes.

- Check for mail: There is always some sort of delivery or box to be opened and put away.

- Learn through hands-on training with the equipment.

STATION UTILITIES AND ADDITIONAL INFORMATION

By now, you have probably realized that the station duties mostly consist of cooking and cleaning. While that is true, there are some other aspects you need to be aware of. You really need to know about the whole station, including:

- The phone numbers and access codes to the gates and doors.

- Where all the utilities are located. This includes the electrical panel, gas shut off, and water shut off.

- Where the backup emergency generator is and how to use, service, and test it.

- Where the hot water heater and the air conditioner are located.

- How to use all the radio equipment and what it is for. We once had a rookie shut down the station's main radio because the chatter was too loud at night. The problem was, that particular radio unit controls the station dispatch system. The crew missed several calls that night and even though they were well rested, the rookie had to learn a tough lesson in the morning.

- The proper, professional way your department answers a telephone. Always be the first one to answer the phone. There should be a race for the phone. (Seriously, I've seen wrestling matches over a phone call, taking out trash, soap buckets, mops, brooms, paper towel rolls, vacuums, and car keys.) Don't let someone else answer your phone!

- All the functions of the phone so you don't hang up on the Fire Chief. Whoops!

- The right way to answer the front door (very similar to answering the phone).

And in addition to these, you should be the first point of contact for all station visitors. When someone comes to the station, you should try to handle their questions or business to the best of your ability before getting someone else involved. If a station tour has been scheduled, you can be sure it's going to land squarely on your shoulders. It's a good idea to think about that situation before your guests arrive. There is material out there on how to handle a station visit, so be sure to do some research before you give your first tour or you may end up making a rookie mistake.

A ROOKIE MISTAKE

HERE is an example of a station visit gone wrong, proving why preparation and a little common sense are essential.

We had a couple of classes of second graders visiting our station one day. It was a pretty typical situation. The rookie had walked the students, parents, and teachers through the station, pointing out the interesting items and making the typical corny school-visit jokes.

After the walk through the station, he took them outside to show them the department's newest fire engine. He had them all lined up in our freshly redone front yard. The public works department had just planted a California native, water-friendly yard, fresh with about three dump trucks full of decomposed granite (DG is like the infield of a baseball diamond). Our rookie then sat the kids down in the fresh DG and showed them how he put his turnouts on. He showed them his breather and his thermal imager. Then he decided to show them our gasoline-powered positive pressure ventilation fan.

He fired it up, pointed it at the group, and gave it some throttle. It instantly started sucking the pea-sized rocks and dirt off the ground and shooting them out of the fan toward the crowd of children and their teachers. Everyone started ducking and running for cover! The whole thing lasted about a minute, but that lapse of common sense will stay with that rookie for his entire career. We were lucky that the only thing hurt was some rookie pride. The point is, always be at the top of your game, use common sense, and know your equipment.

TESTING

As a probationary firefighter, you are fighting for your job every day. This means that if a department feels that you are a cocky little punk (attitude), if you have a poor work ethic (effort), or you're not a productive member of the team (teamwork), then they can fire you. (Did you notice which three words were in parentheses?) As a probationary firefighter, you are an at-will employee. That means you aren't entitled to the same rights as the other sworn-in, non-probationary fire department employees.

Even though the same rights do not protect you as the rest of the department, the administrative staff still needs to be able to prove that any termination of an at-will employee was done for legal reasons. Meaning, they can't fire you because of your race, color, religion, gender, age (for workers over 40), pregnancy, citizenship, familial status, disability status, veteran status, genetic information, or national origin. All of these are considered protected classes under the United States federal anti-discrimination law.

The department needs to have solid documentation to show that terminating a probationary employee was for good reason. If the release of an employee comes into question, the department should be able to prove that they did everything within reason to help train, coach, and counsel the probationer, and that the employee was still unsuccessful at meeting the department's standards.

You may be asking yourself, "What does this have to do with my testing?" The answer is, testing is your first and most frequent opportunity for documentation.

Testing is the department's way of seeing whether you have what it takes to make it as a firefighter. It's how they find out whether you are capable of learning and performing under pressure. It also shows you're willing to put in the time and effort to keep your position.

Most fire departments will break your rookie testing down into three different categories. These categories are designed to test your book smarts, your equipment knowledge, and your ability to perform a task.

BONUS TIP

I would suggest focusing your studies on tools and equipment while on shift. This will allow you valuable time to actually be hands-on with your subject. You should leave the written materials for quiet hours and studying at home.

THE WRITTEN TEST

You should understand the written test-taking process by now. You have probably taken hundreds of written tests as you've made your way through grade school and college, paramedic school, or a fire academy.

People do learn at different speeds, but if you study the information long enough, then you should be able to pass, plain and simple. Just make sure you have a full understanding of what the test will be covering. Most department tests come straight from the *IFSTA Essentials*, department policy, city information (streets, district boundaries, city council members, fire station locations, phone numbers, etc.), or departmental equipment manuals.

If you have any questions about your tests, ask your training officer for a list of study materials or where you should start gathering your information. The previous rookie class is also a valuable resource that should be able to point you in the right direction. Nothing is worse than assuming you are studying the right material only to find out during the test that you were wrong. I also recommend knowing your department's failure protocol (i.e., what is the passing score, is there a retake policy, etc.) Hopefully, they never need to use it on your behalf, but it's always good to know where you stand.

THE COMPANY SCHOOL

THE company school wasn't designed to create a feeling of terror and panic in the heart of a rookie, but it usually does. In my opinion, the company school is the hardest and most stressful part of rookie testing. Its purpose is to test your skills and knowledge by having you give a presentation on a specific subject or piece of equipment, with your crew as your audience.

As a new rookie, this will most likely be the toughest audience you've ever spoken in front of. In a typical class or presentation, you're teaching a subject that you are confident in to people who are not as familiar with the subject as you are. So you may be able to B.S. or "wing it" if you get into a little bit of trouble remembering a fact or two.

However, in a company school, you have to approach the presentation as if your audience knows nothing about the subject, when in fact, they are the experts on the subject. B.S. doesn't stand a chance here. You need to be on top of your game and give a knockout performance every time. If you don't, they will tear you up. But the good news is, I can teach you how to put together a solid presentation outline that will be easily transferable from one company school to the next.

Your presentation will cover a ton of information. At first, you may feel like trying to remember a script word for word. I don't recommend this, because of the large amount of information you need to remember and the possibility of interruptions from calls and people coming and going. Most scripted company schools tend to get choppy, be hard to follow, or ramble on forever.

Instead, you need to have a generic bullet point format that you can apply to all of your company schools. A set format takes away the stress of building a custom presentation for each of your company schools and allows you to simply plug in new information and specifications.

I recommend using the basic categories of what, where, when, how, safety, and maintenance to build your format, and following each one with three to seven bullet points. Bullet points are easy to remember, help you to stay on course, and allow you to cover all your information without sounding robotic and nervous.

So, let's take a closer look at the questions:

What:

This is where you will introduce your subject. If you are doing a company school on a piece of equipment, include the make, model, and all the specific parts and specifications. If you are presenting a certain subject matter, this is where you describe what it is that you are doing.

Here is an example using a piece of equipment:

The Rescue 42 Telecrib composite strut system is an easy-to-use, lightweight, collapsible support system designed to stabilize vehicles and light structures. The struts are made of a lightweight, strong, composite material that is impervious to moisture and most chemicals. The struts are electrically non-conductive to provide a layer of protection to rescuers working around live electricity.

The working capacity of the rescue struts is on a slide scale with the greatest load capacity measured in the fully retracted mode at eighteen thousand pounds and the lowest rated capacity measured in the fully extended setting at four thousand pounds. Please see the load table located on each strut for exact weight ratings.

Our inventory consists of:

- 2 short struts = 26"–67"

- 2 long struts = 38"–103"

- 4 base plates

And so on and so forth until each piece of equipment and accessory is labeled.

Where:

This is a simpler question and generally pertains to equipment, so answer by stating all of the locations where the item may be found.

When:

This is your opportunity to showcase your knowledge on the tactical or operational uses of a piece of equipment. For example, if your company school is on a chainsaw, you could say, "We use our Stihl MS 461 rescue chain saw during vertical ventilation operations. As a member of the truck company, we would cut at minimum a 16-square-foot heat hole at the highest point over the fire to release the super-heated smoke and gasses from the structure, making it more tenable for victims and firefighters." Just be careful not to go off on too much of a tangent—be prepared to answer any questions on anything you talk about. Don't dig yourself a hole.

How:

This is the technical part of the company school. Sometimes this is an easy question and other times it's not. Try to break it down to its individual components. Let's use an SCBA as an example. I would explain the path the air takes through the entire breather, starting as if the air was outside. How does it get pressurized and put in the tank? How does it make its way through the hoses and regulators? What do the regulators do to the air and at what pressures? How does it enter your mask? How does it exit your mask? Answering all of these questions will provide a great explanation of how your breather works. Basically, you need to explain every point of contact the air makes with the SCBA.

Safety:

This section should be in every company school. It lets your company officer know that you are a safety-minded person, and that you understand the dangers present and are able to use each piece of equipment safely.

Maintenance:

This topic is designed to show that you know how to take care of your equipment and keep it in a state of readiness. You should talk about your responsibility of after-use maintenance and how often scheduled maintenance is needed. Your department may also have maintenance policies that you should reference.

You should also have some sort of visual aid for the company school. The best visual aid is the actual subject matter. Bring the chainsaw or breather into the class. Take the class to the apparatus floor if you are teaching them about a larger equipment system. You should get hands-on with the equipment and show the class how it's put into operation. These company schools are also a very good refresher course for crew members that haven't seen the equipment in use for a while. Seeing a well-prepared hands-on demonstration benefits everyone.

Having some sort of handout for the crew, or a PowerPoint presentation, is another great way to showcase your skills and knowledge. This also gives the crew something to do other than stare at you and wait for you to make a mistake. If you make it "kinda shiny," it will hold their attention. If a member of your crew happens to slip out of consciousness, that person can look at the handout and see what they missed, rather than punish you with questions at the end of your presentation on material you have already covered. It also shows that you put a lot of time and effort into your company school and they may appreciate the effort.

If you do have visual aids as part of your presentation, make sure not to read directly from them. You are supposed to memorize the material, not read it from a projector or handout. You should stand with your back to the PowerPoint presentation or white board and rarely point to it, so there is no doubt that you have memorized your material.

Always close out your company school with a question and answer session. I like to call this part of the presentation "stump the chump." Stump the chump is a good indication of how your company school went. Here is a little tip to keep in mind: The person asking the question isn't asking for their benefit. They already know the answer and are only asking because they feel you should have included that information in your company school.

When you are asked a question you don't know the answer to, never make up an answer. The correct response is, "I'm not sure, but I will find out and get back to you with that answer, sir." This next part is important: It is imperative that you actually do the research and get the correct answer back to that person in a timely matter (usually by the end of the day). Don't ask someone else at your station for the answer, and don't forget that you made that promise, because they won't.

If your crew has no questions at the end of your presentation, then you should congratulate yourself on a job well done! (Or be worried because you put the entire crew to sleep.)

MANIPULATIVE SKILLS

I believe the most important tests are the manipulative kind for one simple reason. It's easy to read a book or study a certain subject, but when it's time to get dirty, can you actually do what is expected of you? Can your Captain trust that when you get off that engine and are given a task, you can complete it in a timely manner and not hurt yourself or anyone else? *Manipulative tests are the best way to prove your competency to your new crew.*

Manipulative skills take time and practice to master. Most of this time and practice should have already taken place in your training tower. By the time you hit the floor as a firefighter, you should be confident and capable in performing your skills.

There are two ways we test manipulative skills. The first is the monthly skills sign-off that is done at the company level. These skills will vary from month to month until all pertinent skills have been demonstrated. Sign-off skills are your responsibility to complete, and no one is likely to remind you to get them done. You also need to keep in mind that with everything expected of you on a daily basis, the shifts go by really fast. Make sure you stay up to date and are diligent in completing your skills on time.

The second way to test your manipulative skills is the cumulative test. Many departments give their rookies cumulative tests at the six- and twelve-month points of probation. These tests are highly important, as they are markers of how well you are progressing and how well you have retained previous skills and information. Do not take these tests lightly—many departments use them as trigger points for releasing rookies who are having trouble.

If you are performing poorly on tests or your work ethic isn't up to par, then you should expect all of that to be documented by your Captain or training staff. And as you learned earlier, documentation will make the department's case if they are looking to terminate an employee who isn't meeting their standards.

After everything you have accomplished to get to this point, the only reason for not passing a test is that you didn't prepare properly. And that's on you.

CHOW

"The shit runs downhill"

...AND as a rookie, you are at the very bottom of that hill with your arms wide open. And in this case, the chow is the shit.

Although everybody enjoys eating, not everybody enjoys cooking. In your position, if no one else volunteers to cook, that responsibility falls on you. Feeding the crew is the most time-consuming part of probation and it is never-ending, consuming 3 to 4 hours of *every* shift. In the kitchen, you will become a master of accepting criticism and managing your time and stress levels, and if you pay attention, you may even learn how to cook.

But before you can start cooking, you need to decide on what you are going to eat. When I first started, I didn't have a lot of recipes to pull from. I would come up with a menu the day before my shift so I wouldn't have to stress over it. Always be ready for the inevitable question, "What's for chow?"

The answer to that question is never "I don't know." Instead, ask yourself, "Do I have time to cook?" If you do, then respond by offering one of the pre-planned meals you thought of the day before. If there isn't time to cook, then you should start to list all the local places categorized by type of food. For example:

Capt.:
    What's for lunch, rookie?

Rookie:

Well sir, I would be happy to cook burgers for lunch, but it seems like we may be short on time sir.

Capt.:

You're right, that training really killed our morning.

Rookie:

Well sir, we could pick up Mexican, sandwiches, burgers...

Capt.:

Let's do sandwiches.

Rookie:

Sounds good. We could go to Subway, or that local deli we went to last Monday.

Capt.:

Yeah, let's head over to that deli, I liked their chicken salad.

This situation could happen at any time, so it's important to always have some sort of cash or card on you.

Typically, lunch is at noon and dinner is at six. If you have time to cook at the station, then you will need to shop for groceries. I would suggest you shop at least two hours before mealtime. Some stations are lucky enough to be located near a grocery store. This gives you the ability to inform your Captain of your plan to go shopping, take a radio, walk over, and shop by yourself.

Other stations are not quite as lucky. They need to load the entire crew up and drive to the grocery store. If this is the situation you are in, be prepared to shop for both meals at the same time. Although this will take more planning, it will save your crew the hassle of going to the store twice, and trust me, they will appreciate it.

Sometimes training or calls may delay or completely prevent you from cooking. This is just part of life as a firefighter, so get used to it. Most people are usually understanding of legitimate reasons for chow being late. It is the illegitimate reasons that they will harass you about. Poor planning is not an excuse for late chow.

At some point, everyone will decide to order out for chow. When this happens and you are still in the station, you will most likely want to call ahead and place the order. Most stations have a kitchen drawer that is full of local restaurant menus. When you're new, this can help give you some ideas of local places that are acceptable to order from.

When ordering out, grab whichever menu you decide and walk around the station with your pen and paper and write down everyone's order. Don't forget to invite everyone who is at your station, including battalion chiefs, dispatchers, mechanics, or family members who may be visiting.

When picking up your order from the restaurant, make sure you double-check it. It's embarrassing to get back to the station and realize they didn't give you the chief's breakfast burrito. If this does happen, the appropriate kitchen etiquette would be to offer him yours.

THE CHOW BOX

Depending on your station, you may have a collection of money to be used for shopping. This cache of cash is often used in the larger stations that have an expensive daily food bill. No one should be expected to front a large amount of money for chow, and using a box is easier than collecting money before you go shopping each time. We call ours the "chow box." Where I work, each shift has their own chow box, and the rookies are usually responsible for managing it. After dinner, the rookie tallies the receipts to come up with a total owed per person for the day. No matter what the cost of chow is, people will always complain that it's way too much. "Twelve bucks for that slop! You've got to be joking!"

If someone forgets to pay or doesn't have cash on hand for the chow box, an IOU is acceptable if paid back within a reasonable amount of time. As a rookie, you should avoid IOUs at all costs. For the others, make sure you document the IOUs and the amount of cash in the box to help keep it balanced. You don't want to deplete your shift's chow box, so you need to charge the crew what you spend. At the end of the night, you need to make sure the chow box is locked and stored away where it belongs.

If you work at a smaller station, you may not have a chow box. In this case, you may need to front the money for the groceries. Then at the end of the day, collect what you are owed. Sometimes, when you're new, it's awkward to ask someone to pay you back for a meal. I've found that the easiest way to collect money (personally or for the chow box) is to write on the station whiteboard who owes what. Make sure you do this sooner rather than later to give everyone plenty of time to pay. Once a person pays, they erase their own name. If someone hasn't paid by the end of the night, it's usually because they forgot. If you ask politely, they should jump right up and get your money. Everyone knows that they are expected to pay for their meals, so collecting shouldn't be a too much of a problem.

Rookie:
   Excuse me sir.

Me:
   What's up?

Rookie:
   I just wanted to remind you that dinner was $8.

Me:
   Oh yeah, I'll get it for you right after *Point Break* is over.

Two hours later.

Rookie:
   Sir, I don't want to bother you, but I noticed *Point Break* is over.

Me:
   Oh yeah, I'll get it right now. Hey guys, pause *Tombstone*. I've got to get junior his money before he breaks my legs.

THE PANTRY

SLUSH, staples, or whatever your department calls it, the pantry is all the non-personal food that is kept in the kitchen cupboards. This will vary from station to station but usually includes all of the coffee, condiments, cooking oils, crackers, dressings, butter, rice, and pancake mix. And that's just a sample of a much longer list. These items need to be replenished and kept track of.

Usually, there is one person at each station in charge of doing the slush. This is actually a fairly large responsibility. It involves keeping the pantry stocked, shopping, keeping a reserve of goods, and collecting and spending the money of each employee who works at that station. While I think a more experienced person should handle this responsibility, it may fall on your shoulders as the rookie. If this is a task assigned to you, accept it and take it seriously.

There are a few ways a station may collect for their slush fund. One way is to collect up front from each person at the beginning of each month. The other way is to collect a small portion of money each shift by adding it to the cost of the chow bill. If you happen to be in charge of your shift's chow box, make sure this money gets collected and paid to the person in charge of slush.

FIREHOUSE KITCHEN TRADITIONS

As we know, the fire service is steeped in tradition. A good majority of these traditions have to do with the firehouse kitchen and the food that gets prepared in it.

This starts on a firefighter's first day with a new crew. The newcomer will cook a special meal as a way to introduce himself or herself. Firefighters will also cook a special meal on their last day with a crew as a way of saying thanks.

Most departments I know of have a traditional Saturday or Sunday brunch. This meal takes a little extra time to prepare and is expected earlier than lunch during the week. Start planning for the brunch shopping trip as soon as the engine checkout is done in the morning. If you are having a busy morning and can't make brunch, then you should have a good local breakfast spot on speed dial as a backup.

Another great tradition in my department takes place after returning from a large fire early in the morning. At our firehouse, we make a big batch of pancakes and everyone is expected to sit and eat. This is one of my favorite firehouse traditions because everyone is excited, smells like smoke, and is starving after a fire. It's a great time to sit around the table and shoot it. If your department doesn't have this tradition, you should start it.

THE ALMIGHTY DESSERT

DESSERT will be given all kinds of nicknames by different departments. We call ours "pus." We call it pus because if you eat too much, you get all fat and pus-like. Dessert is almost like currency in the firehouse. It can be used to pay debts or given as a reward. There are several traditions that revolve around dessert.

First of all, you should be aware that you never show up for a station visit empty-handed. The amount of time and thought you put into your station visit pus is a direct indication of how much you value and respect the time and effort the crew is giving to you. Do not show up with that cheap one-gallon bucket of ice cream. No one eats that. No one eats those off-brand soggy Drumsticks, either. Grab the name-brand good stuff or do something original! Trust me, it's better that I tell you now.

Another firehouse tradition is the first-time pus, which happens when you do something substantial for the first time in your career. Here is an example:

Engineer:
Hey rookie, was that your first car fire?

Rookie:
Yes sir, it was!

Engineer:
Ice cream!

Now you have to buy the station ice cream. That's just how it works.

There is also the media-driven dessert that is owed any time you are unlucky enough to be on the news or in the newspaper. Even though this is exciting the first few times, let it be known that pus is owed to your station. This may explain why you see firefighters running away from cameras and the press.

If a certain person or crew has to clean up a mistake you made or finds some of your equipment you've lost, you owe pus. For example, if you go on a medical aid and end up leaving some equipment on scene and you and your crew have to go back for it, you owe them dessert. If another crew brings it to you, then you owe that crew dessert.

Then there is overtime. Some departments have a tradition that the over-timers pay for dessert. It is up to them to pay for it, but it may be up to the rookie to actually go get it and/or bake it.

KITCHEN RULES FOR THE ROOKIE COOK

By this point, you can see that the kitchen in a firehouse is a very busy place. As the default shift cook, you will probably be in the kitchen more than most of the other crewmembers—get used to it. Since you will be spending so much time in there, let's quickly go over some etiquette and cooking tips that will help you play the game in the kitchen.

- The cook is responsible for making sure there is enough food for everyone who is eating that day. That means you should serve yourself last to make sure there is enough food to go around.

- If another unit is stationed with you (paramedic ambulance or truck company) and they are not at the station when it's time to eat, it is up to the cook to try and preserve that food to the best of his or her ability. For example, cover hot food with aluminum foil, and don't put hot meat on a salad; leave it on the side. That way, if someone can't eat right away, their lettuce doesn't get wilted and nasty. Also, if another unit at your house has to run a call during dinner, it is polite to cover their food if they don't get a chance to do it.

- The cook should sit down to eat last, but as the rookie, you should be the first one up to start cleaning. Sometimes this is difficult to do, so you need to eat fast.

- As a rookie, you should not be watching TV. This includes during meals. If you have a hard time with this, you should sit with your back to the TV.

- If the phone rings during chow, you need to be the first to answer it. If your station has a portable phone, go grab it before you sit down and put it in your pocket.

- Put up a fight to be in the suds after meals. Do the dishes at all costs.

- Don't let anyone else take out the trash, and always be the first one to the mop. I know this seems impossible, and it may be, but if you work hard and attempt to do all these things, your crew will notice and gain respect for you and your work ethic.

- Always buy at least one extra package when cooking bacon. It will disappear as you cook it. I would also recommend having a dedicated bacon shirt, because if you don't, you will ruin a different shirt each time you cook.

- Don't open chip bags before lunch. Hide them in a cabinet or just buy an extra bag because they won't make it to lunchtime.

- If your station has a rice cooker, use it. They are awesome! You'll see. They cook while you're on call!

- Fire station knives are always dull. Learn how to sharpen knives properly, and then spend a little time doing so.

- Always be aware of what's going on in the kitchen and always offer to help. It's expected that you will.

- Coffee, coffee, coffee, coffee, coffee, coffee, coffee, coffee, coffee, and more coffee!

- Don't ever use frozen hamburger patties.

- Don't wash your hands in the kitchen sink after a call. Do that in the bathroom first.

- Don't forget to run the dishwasher if you are low on dishes.

- And most importantly, don't forget to turn off all flames when responding to a call while cooking. You never know how long you will be gone and you don't want to respond back to your station for a structure fire.

Some days, you may just be too busy or overwhelmed to think about a meal plan, or maybe you have run out of new ideas. For those days, I have included some of my favorite firehouse recipes at the end of the book (see page 57).

EMERGENCY RESPONSE

"It's time to go work"

RESPONDING to emergency calls is the one part of the job that you have actually trained for. The fire academy, EMT classes, and paramedic school have all prepared you for this part of your career. My goal is a little different from theirs. Instead of teaching you the manipulative skills needed to do the job, I'm going to give you some insight on what your role will be and how to play the game on scene.

Your Captain has a job. His job is to make the plan of action. Your job is to make that plan happen quickly and safely. By this point, you should be competent enough with your skills to get by with little direct supervision. On a fire call, the direction you get from your Captain will sound something like this: "Throw a ladder, I'm going to see what we've got and I'll be back." He's not going to hold your hand and say, "I need you to take the twenty-four foot extension ladder and place it against that building right there. I want it about eight feet from the corner and make sure it's not directly in front of any doors or windows. I want there to be three to five rungs above the roof line and make sure the climbing angle is seventy degrees. When you're done with that, start grabbing the ventilation equipment because that's the next step." When you can anticipate the needs of the call, that is when you become truly useful.

As a rookie on scene, you need to keep your mouth closed and your eyes and ears open. Learn through experiences, watch the senior firefighters, and learn something from every call.

When it comes to questions like "Sir, what was the reason for this?" or "Should I have done that differently?" ask them on the way back to the station house, **not on an active scene.** The only questions you should be asking on scene are those that clarify what your orders are. Just remember, your job is to work hard to make the Captain's plan a success.

Each fire department will have its own set of policies pertaining to operations. Before you start running calls, you need to know what your department's policies, procedures, and operational directives are. State and county-run health departments regulate our actions on medical emergencies. These regulations must be strictly followed. Also, each department has a specific culture when it comes to running calls. You will have to learn your department's cultural practices for yourself. Pay attention and you will pick up on these quickly. Listen to the advice your crew is giving you and turn that advice into action.

Even though every department is unique, there are some practices that are universal. For example, the young backs should always offer to do the heavy lifting. The rookies should be lifting the gurney and carrying as much equipment as possible. You are the hands of the crew! If there is a vomitus patient or a smelly GI bleed response, as the FNG you should be the first one in to help. Always follow your Captain off the rig, no matter where he is going. If he doesn't need your help, he will tell you to stay put. Also, always try to anticipate the needs of the engineer and back him up when needed. It will be expected.

ATTITUDE TOWARD CALLS

YOU may hear the older firefighters complain a bit if a call comes in at a mealtime or if they've just gotten into bed for the night. A lot of times, they will complain for no good reason at all. Not you, though. You don't get to complain. Don't ever let the crew hear you complain about going on a call. Even if it's the third time to the same house, on the same shift, and everyone else is complaining. If you complain about calls early in your career, it sends the message that you aren't excited to be there. You're telling everyone that you're tired of this already and you would rather be doing something else. Maybe that's true, but remember, people like helping people who are excited and happy about what they are doing. Excited, happy people don't complain. Keep it to yourself.

So, when the alarm sounds, smile and stabilize whatever it is that you are doing as quickly as possible and get to your apparatus. Open the bay doors and start preparing for your response. When you hear what kind of emergency you are responding to, you should start thinking, "How am I going to prepare myself?" and, "What personal protective equipment will I need?" If you have any questions about what PPE you should be wearing, you can just look and see what the Captain or other firefighters are wearing. If you're still unsure, just ask.

While en route, try to anticipate the early needs of the call. If you are pulling up to a car fire, you may want to put your mask on just as the rig is pulling up. I actually missed out on my first car fire because someone else had his mask on and was ready to fight fire, and I wasn't. Another time I wish I had been a little faster, we were first on scene to a single-family residence that was well involved with fire. I got out of the rig and went to pull our pre-connected quick attack line. As I pulled the hose cover down, both transverse hose beds were empty. It turns out there was a paramedic squad on the other side just waiting for our engine to pull up. As soon as the airbrakes were set, they grabbed both of my lines and deployed them. It's hard to stay professional when you want to wrestle the nozzle out of a paramedic's hand, but on the front lawn of a burning home with the homeowners watching isn't the time or place for that type of behavior.

When you are en route to a more technical call, you may want to go over in your mind what equipment could be needed and where it is located. There is nothing worse than having to open all the compartment doors looking for a tool, especially when there is a crowd of people recording you with their cell phones and there is a person pinned under a car. Be prepared so others don't have to suffer—mere seconds can mean life or death.

CREW SAFETY

CREW safety comes from proper training, situational awareness, and common sense. We all need to be safe on scene. I have told you that as a rookie you should be on the quiet side and listen most of the time. *Not when it comes to safety.* When it comes to safety—if you see something, **say something.** There is no rank when it comes to safety.

TRAINING

TRAINING is important! The first step in crew safety is training. It allows us to learn and practice with each other in a controlled environment. Training is what gives you that feeling in your gut when something just isn't right. It's also what gives you your reactionary instinct when you don't have enough time to think things through, but need to take action.

Just like calls, though, training will be complained about. Also just like calls, you don't get to complain as a rookie. As a rookie, you will be expected to do everything to the best of your ability on the training ground. When you are training, academy rules apply: No walking, stay hydrated, and so on.

SITUATIONAL AWARENESS

IN the fire service, we need to have a heightened sense of our surroundings in order to stay safe. The term "situational awareness" seems pretty self-explanatory, but it is actually tough to achieve 100 percent of the time.

Our situations are always changing. We may go from a sick person to a structure fire. A traffic accident to an electrical short. After a while, working all of these different types of emergencies seems normal to us and we can get complacent. When people get complacent, they lose their situational awareness, and that's when people get hurt.

Another time you may lose situational awareness is when you are fighting a structure fire. It's easy to get tunnel vision toward the active fire. We call this the "moth to flame" syndrome. When this happens, you completely lose awareness of everything going on around you as you focus on the actual fire. This can be extremely dangerous, and to maintain your safety, it's important to stop and check your surroundings occasionally while firefighting operations are being conducted.

You also need to know that dispatch doesn't always get it right. They work hard to provide good information to the units in the field, but sometimes the dispatch center isn't able to get all the pertinent information from the caller. Sometimes the caller gives a range of information from bad to none. For this reason, you can never be 100 percent sure of the situation you are walking into. You need to be ready for anything.

Another problem our profession deals with is agitated or violent people on scene. When this happens, the police should make first contact. If you are aware of this at the time of dispatch, your Captain should request or confirm that PD is responding and your crew should stage out until PD clears the scene.

Even if the police make first contact, you will still need to learn how to isolate yourself from agitated patients. Don't ever let a patient grab you or any member of your crew. Remember, we are family, and family comes first. We watch our family's backs.

COMMON SENSE

SOMETIMES, common sense doesn't seem so common. This holds true for both the citizens and the fire department personnel. If I could just get rookies to stop doing the following few things, I could retire a happy man:

- When you are on a call and you are working out of a medical box or toolbox, leave it open. When you are done, close the lid and **latch it!** Never shut the lid without latching it! There is nothing worse than picking up a box that is closed but not latched and turning the entire contents of the box into a yard sale all over the scene.

- Don't set your equipment on someone's car or furniture. The equipment should be placed on the ground to avoid damaging property. I guarantee you wouldn't set your medical box down on your mom's kitchen table!

- Make sure to shut the door every time you get out of a vehicle. The engineer can't drive or reposition the rig with your door open.

- Do your best not to step in blood or vomit. When you walk through blood or other body fluids, you end up tracking it into the rig and back into the station. Seems simple, right?

- Don't set your equipment in blood or vomit. Again, seems like a no-brainer, but it happens all the time when new rookies get focused on patient care.

- Don't grab equipment with bloody gloves, if you can avoid it. You should keep an extra set of gloves in your boxes just in case you need to switch them out.

Sometimes you can't avoid getting blood and guts on your equipment. When this happens, make sure you thoroughly decontaminate it. Failing to clean it properly is not only gross, but also a safety concern. When people forget or don't do the responsible thing and decontaminate properly, it puts the entire crew at risk for communicable diseases. The people who use the equipment after you assume that it is clean. If you haven't properly decontaminated it, they become contaminated and don't even know it.

THE EVER-READY ROOKIE

THE fire department's job is to mitigate hazards that pose a threat to life, environment, or property. In order for us to do that, we need to respond quickly and keep our equipment in a constant state of readiness. The best way to stay ready is to complete a thorough morning check out and keep a mental list of supplies and equipment that were used on your last call. As soon as you are able to, you need to restock those supplies and get your equipment back to its "fire ready" status.

You need to do whatever it takes to keep your apparatus completely operational. This may include the complete break down and cleaning of a chainsaw at 3 am. If your equipment isn't ready for the next call, you will be putting the public, your fire family, and your job at risk. That's unacceptable.

Aside from operational reasons, there is another purpose for keeping your apparatus clean and ready to respond. At the end of your shift, you will be able to pass on an engine, truck, or paramedic unit that was well taken care of while you were responsible for it. This is also known as **PRIDE!**

IF <u>YOU</u> NEED HELP

In our line of work, we see some pretty horrible things. I know we are all tough people and don't ever see ourselves needing help, but some day you might. It's good to know that there are people who can help you with personal issues. The culture of some departments can make this a difficult task, and as a rookie, you may not want to use an employee assistance program (EAP) out of fear of being found out or having your reputation damaged.

You should know these programs are completely confidential. If you are having trouble getting past a traumatic event, you can ask someone in the department you feel comfortable with how to access an EAP. You can also contact your human resources department. They should be able to point you in the right direction and get you the help you need. Your department chaplain is also a good resource for difficult times.

An EAP can be offered through the department, city, or district you work for, and is typically free of charge.

AFTER PROBATION

"Level up"

CONGRATULATIONS! You made it through probation! Now get back to work.

I wish I could say that transitioning from a rookie to a confident, experienced firefighter is a simple, straightforward line to walk, but it's not. You are walking more of a zigzag pattern lying over a straight line. The straight line is what I like to call the "comfort line." Here is how it really works.

You will finish probation and in the next few months, you will start to get a little more comfortable in your station. You may not run for the phone anymore or you may hang out drinking coffee longer than you should. This might go on for a little while until somebody says, "Hey, I overheard the Captains talking at shift change. They said you are sure getting comfortable. Playing basketball all the time and walking around in your slippers." Then wham-o, just like that, you get all nervous again and suddenly change your whole routine. It's back to that old-fashioned, nervous, rookie way of life.

Then a couple weeks down the road someone else will ask, "Why are you so nervous all the time? You need to relax a little. You're not on probation anymore and everybody kind of thinks you need to loosen up. That's how people get to know the real you." Then you think, "Well, that does seem true. I better start easing up a little." And the whole process starts over again. Each time you go from relaxed mode to rookie mode, the swing gets less and less extreme, until you even out onto the comfort line. That's when all the hard work truly pays off.

And then there is the other issue: While you are technically not on probation any longer, you may still be the lowest in seniority on your crew. And even if there is another class of recruits beneath you on the seniority list, it usually takes being on the job a minimum of three to five years until you are totally comfortable and completely accepted by your department. You may be able to sit in the chairs and watch TV or wash your truck occasionally, but remember what I said earlier—the shit runs downhill.

RECIPES

There are a million different firehouse cookbooks out there. This isn't one of them. I just wanted to give you a few of my old faithful recipes.

THE CLASSIC FIREHOUSE LUNCH: TACO SALAD

Where I come from, this is a classic. You just can't go wrong with TS.

Feeds about 10 people

- 2 ½ cups white rice
- 6 pounds ground beef or turkey
- 6 ounces taco seasoning
- 16-ounce block cheddar cheese
- Two 9 1/4-ounce bags of Fritos
- One 9 1/4-ounce bag of Chili Cheese Fritos
- 3 heads romaine lettuce, shredded
- 3 large tomatoes, chopped
- 4-5 avocados, sliced (optional)
- 1 bunch fresh cilantro leaves, chopped
- Ranch dressing
- Hot sauce or salsa
- One 30-ounce can black beans

Get the rice started first, and cook it according to the package directions. Heat a large skillet over medium heat. Add the meat and taco seasoning and cook, stirring occasionally, until the meat is cooked through, about 10 minutes. Shred the cheese and place in a bowl. Place the Fritos, lettuce, tomatoes, avocado, and cilantro in separate bowls. When the rice is done, drain the beans, add them to the rice, and stir to warm the beans. Set up the rice and beans, meat, toppings, and condiments in an assembly line. Chow's on!

PEPPER-JACK CHICKEN SANDWICHES

A new twist on an old classic.

Feeds 10 people

- 10 chicken breasts
- 10 whole green chiles from a can
- 10 slices pepper jack cheese
- 10 high-quality hamburger buns

- 1 head romaine lettuce leaves
- 3 tomatoes, sliced crosswise
- 1 large onion, sliced into rings
- Three 7-ounce bags of chips
- Fruit of your choosing

Prepare the grill. Grill the chicken breasts for about 7-8 minutes on each side. When your chicken is nearly cooked, place one chile pepper on each breast, cover with a slice of cheese, and keep cooking until the cheese has melted. (You may want to ask around first, as some people may not want cheese.) Set out the chicken, buns, and toppings so everyone can assemble their own sandwiches, and serve the chips and fruit on the side.

PULLED PORK SANDWICHES AND TOTS

This Crock-Pot recipe requires 6 to 8 hours of cooking time. This meal is great because after a long day, it's ready to go and you're a hero!

Feeds about 10 people

- 1 medium head cabbage, shredded, or one 20-ounce bag mixed green and red shredded cabbage

- 2 carrots, grated

- 1 onion, diced

- 1 cup vinegar

- ¾ cup vegetable oil

- 1 cup sugar

- 1 teaspoon salt

- About 10 pounds pork tenderloin

- ¾ cup steak seasoning

- 2–3 cups brewed coffee

- 1 ½ cups barbecue sauce

- Two to three 32-ounce bags frozen tater tots

- 2 burger buns per person

Mix the shredded cabbage, carrots, and onion in a large bowl. Add the vinegar, oil, sugar, and salt. Mix and refrigerate for 5 to 6 hours, or until dinner is ready. Rub the meat with a generous amount of steak seasoning. Put the meat in the slow cooker and add enough black coffee to fill the cooker by about 2 to 3 inches. Cook on medium for 5 to 6 hours, until the meat pulls apart easily. Drain about three quarters of the juice from the slow cooker, then add 1 1/2 cups barbecue sauce. Cook on medium for approximately 1 more hour. Meanwhile, heat the tater tots according to the package directions. Serve the pulled pork on the buns topped with the coleslaw, and "Get your own tots." Chow's on!

CHICKEN BURRITOS

Chicken burritos are great because they work as a meal for the long training day, with 6 hours cooking time in a slow cooker, or they can be a "flash" meal. Flash meals are called "flash" because they are prepared in a flash. Spaghetti is also usually considered a flash meal. Either way you cook it, these burritos are easy.

Feeds about 10 people

- About 10 pounds boneless, skinless chicken breasts (1 pound per person)

- Two 16-ounce jars green salsa (salsa verde)

- 2 ½ cups Spanish rice

- Two 30-ounce cans refried beans

- About 20 burrito-sized tortillas (2 per person)

- 3–4 avocados, sliced

- 1 bunch cilantro leaves, chopped

- 1 head lettuce, shredded

- 2–3 tomatoes, chopped

- 16 ounces shredded cheese

- 4 limes, cut into wedges

- One 11-ounce bag tortilla chips

Slow cooker version:

Put the chicken in the slow cooker and pour the salsa on top. Cook on medium for 6 hours. Near the end of the cooking time, cook the Spanish rice according to the package directions. Heat the beans until warmed through. Warm the tortillas and set out with the chicken, rice, and toppings. Chow's on!

Flash version:

Buy a couple of precooked rotisserie chickens from your local grocery store and shred them up. Cook the Spanish rice according to the package directions, heat the beans until warmed through, and set out the warm tortillas, chicken, rice, and toppings. Chow's on!

DESSERT

REMEMBER how important dessert is in the fire service? Sometimes a situation calls for ice cream, sometimes it calls for pie, and sometimes it calls for a homemade delicious treat the crew hasn't had before. For those situations, you may want to keep these in mind. These are two of my favorite desserts, each for its own delicious reasons.

JUNE BUGS

June bugs are a fairly quick and easy dessert to make and everyone loves them. I have been making these for years on camping trips, but last time I went to the store, I saw the recipe on the side of the Rolo bag and it kind of bummed me out. (I guess you have to give credit, where credit is due.)

- One 20-ounce bag mini pretzels (not the stick version)
- One 12-ounce bag Rolo candies
- One to two 2-ounce bags pecans

Take a cookie sheet or two and cover with foil. Heat the oven to 150 degrees Fahrenheit (65 degrees Celsius), or the lowest temperature available. Spread the pretzels neatly in a single layer on the cookie sheet(s). Place a Rolo on top of each pretzel. Place in the oven for 3 to 5 minutes, just until the Rolo is soft. Remove from the oven and press a pecan half into each Rolo until slightly squashed. Let cool before serving.

KETTLE CORN

Kettle corn is great because it's quick and can usually be made with slush items already at the station. It's also an awesome addition to a station movie night.

- ½ cup sugar
- 1 cup unpopped popcorn kernels

- ½ cup vegetable oil
- Salt

Get a large serving bowl ready before you start cooking. In a tall drinking glass, combine the sugar and kernels. You want to pre-mix the kernels and sugar so they are dropped into the hot oil at the same time. This allows the sugar to turn into a simple syrup and coat the kernels as they pop. Pour the oil into a 12-quart pot with a lid. If you do not have a large enough pot, you will need to cook the popcorn in smaller batches. Heat the oil over medium heat (no higher, or the sugar will burn). Drop three kernels into the heating oil. When the three kernels pop, drop a batch of sugar and kernels into the hot oil and start shaking it around. Keep shaking until the popping begins to slow down, being careful not to burn the popcorn. Remove from the heat and quickly pour into the waiting bowl. Let cool for a couple of minutes, then salt to taste. Repeat with the remaining batches, if necessary.